In the first part of this Workbook,
you are given pictures to color and make stories out of them.
In the second part,
you are provided with a sentence to start your story
and a blank space to draw a sketch regarding it.

Be Creative, Be Imaginative, Be Yourself!
Enjoy Writing, Drawing, and Coloring!

My mum's birthday is next month and I would like to organize a surprise party for her.

This morning, I looked up to the sky and saw a pterodactyl staring down at me.

I woke up from the chirping of the birds and remembered that I was at the mountain lake campsite with my parents.

I was walking back home from school in our quiet neighborhood when a stranger opened the front door of his car and asked me to jump in.

It was a dark, rainy night and the lights went off.

If you were an animal, what would it be?

If you were granted one superpower, what would it be?

If you could visit any planet, which one would it be?

What season do you like most, Summer or Winter? Do you have any hobbies related to these seasons?

Describe the ocean through the eyes of a fish.

When you go out in the garden, do you like to walk in shoes or be barefoot?

Do you like to attract the attention of your friends or not? What do you do about it?

You find a portal in your bedroom. How was it created? Where does it lead?

STUDENT PLAN

TIME	MONDAY	TUESDAY	WEDNESDAY	THURSDAY	FRIDAY

BASIC MULTIPLICATIONS TABLE

1 x
0	x	1	=	0
1	x	1	=	1
2	x	1	=	2
3	x	1	=	3
4	x	1	=	4
5	x	1	=	5
6	x	1	=	6
7	x	1	=	7
8	x	1	=	8
9	x	1	=	9
10	x	1	=	10
11	x	1	=	11
12	x	1	=	12

2 x
0	x	2	=	0
1	x	2	=	2
2	x	2	=	4
3	x	2	=	6
4	x	2	=	8
5	x	2	=	10
6	x	2	=	12
7	x	2	=	14
8	x	2	=	16
9	x	2	=	18
10	x	2	=	20
11	x	2	=	22
12	x	2	=	24

3 x
0	x	3	=	0
1	x	3	=	3
2	x	3	=	6
3	x	3	=	9
4	x	3	=	12
5	x	3	=	15
6	x	3	=	18
7	x	3	=	21
8	x	3	=	24
9	x	3	=	27
10	x	3	=	30
11	x	3	=	33
12	x	3	=	36

4 x
0	x	4	=	0
1	x	4	=	4
2	x	4	=	8
3	x	4	=	12
4	x	4	=	16
5	x	4	=	20
6	x	4	=	24
7	x	4	=	28
8	x	4	=	32
9	x	4	=	36
10	x	4	=	40
11	x	4	=	44
12	x	4	=	48

5 x
0	x	5	=	0
1	x	5	=	5
2	x	5	=	10
3	x	5	=	15
4	x	5	=	20
5	x	5	=	25
6	x	5	=	30
7	x	5	=	35
8	x	5	=	40
9	x	5	=	45
10	x	5	=	50
11	x	5	=	55
12	x	5	=	60

6 x
0	x	6	=	0
1	x	6	=	6
2	x	6	=	12
3	x	6	=	18
4	x	6	=	24
5	x	6	=	30
6	x	6	=	36
7	x	6	=	42
8	x	6	=	48
9	x	6	=	54
10	x	6	=	60
11	x	6	=	66
12	x	6	=	72

7 x
0	x	7	=	0
1	x	7	=	7
2	x	7	=	14
3	x	7	=	21
4	x	7	=	28
5	x	7	=	35
6	x	7	=	42
7	x	7	=	49
8	x	7	=	56
9	x	7	=	63
10	x	7	=	70
11	x	7	=	77
12	x	7	=	84

8 x
0	x	8	=	0
1	x	8	=	8
2	x	8	=	16
3	x	8	=	24
4	x	8	=	32
5	x	8	=	40
6	x	8	=	48
7	x	8	=	56
8	x	8	=	64
9	x	8	=	72
10	x	8	=	80
11	x	8	=	88
12	x	8	=	96

9 x
0	x	9	=	0
1	x	9	=	9
2	x	9	=	18
3	x	9	=	27
4	x	9	=	36
5	x	9	=	45
6	x	9	=	54
7	x	9	=	63
8	x	9	=	72
9	x	9	=	81
10	x	9	=	90
11	x	9	=	99
12	x	9	=	108

10 x
0	x	10	=	0
1	x	10	=	10
2	x	10	=	20
3	x	10	=	30
4	x	10	=	40
5	x	10	=	50
6	x	10	=	60
7	x	10	=	70
8	x	10	=	80
9	x	10	=	90
10	x	10	=	100
11	x	10	=	110
12	x	10	=	120

11 x
0	x	11	=	0
1	x	11	=	11
2	x	11	=	22
3	x	11	=	33
4	x	11	=	44
5	x	11	=	55
6	x	11	=	66
7	x	11	=	77
8	x	11	=	88
9	x	11	=	99
10	x	11	=	110
11	x	11	=	121
12	x	11	=	132

12 x
0	x	12	=	0
1	x	12	=	12
2	x	12	=	24
3	x	12	=	36
4	x	12	=	48
5	x	12	=	60
6	x	12	=	72
7	x	12	=	84
8	x	12	=	96
9	x	12	=	108
10	x	12	=	120
11	x	12	=	132
12	x	12	=	144

93 ENGLISH IRREGULAR VERBS

INFINITIVE	PAST SIMPLE	PAST PARTICIPLE	INFINITIVE	PAST SIMPLE	PAST PARTICIPLE
awake	awoke	awoken	keep	kept	kept
be	was, were	been	know	knew	known
beat	beat	beaten	lay	laid	laid
become	became	become	lead	led	led
begin	began	begun	learn	learned *or* learnt	learned or learnt
bend	bent	bent	leave	left	left
bet	bet	bet	lend	lent	lent
bid	bid	bid	let	let	let
bite	bit	bitten	lie	lay	lain
blow	blew	blown	lose	lost	lost
break	broke	broken	make	made	made
bring	brought	brought	mean	meant	meant
broadcast	broadcast	broadcast	meet	met	met
build	built	built	pay	paid	paid
burn	burned *or* burnt	burned or burnt	put	put	put
buy	bought	bought	read	read	read
catch	caught	caught	ride	rode	ridden
choose	chose	chosen	ring	rang	rung
come	came	come	rise	rose	risen
cost	cost	cost	run	ran	run
cut	cut	cut	say	said	said
dig	dug	dug	see	saw	seen
do	did	done	sell	sold	sold
draw	drew	drawn	send	sent	sent
dream	dreamed *or* dreamt	dreamed or dreamt	show	showed	showed or shown
drive	drove	driven	shut	shut	shut
drink	drank	drunk	sing	sang	sung
eat	ate	eaten	sink	sank	sunk
fall	fell	fallen	sit	sat	sat
feel	felt	felt	sleep	slept	slept
fight	fought	fought	speak	spoke	spoken
find	found	found	spend	spent	spent
fly	flew	flown	stand	stood	stood
forget	forgot	forgotten	stink	stank	stunk
forgive	forgave	forgiven	swim	swam	swum
freeze	froze	frozen	take	took	taken
get	got	got or gotten	teach	taught	taught
give	gave	given	tear	tore	torn
go	went	gone	tell	told	told
grow	grew	grown	think	thought	thought
hang	hung	hung	throw	threw	thrown
have	had	had	understand	understood	understood
hear	heard	heard	wake	woke	woken
hide	hid	hidden	wear	wore	worn
hit	hit	hit	win	won	won
hold	held	held	write	wrote	written
hurt	hurt	hurt			